Effective Social Media Marketing for Restaurants

I0401446

Practical Guide for Food Business Marketing

G. Dellis

Guide to Social Media Marketing for Restaurants

1.Introduction

Social media marketing for restaurants has become an essential element for promoting and growing your business in the food industry. With the rise of social media, people spend more time online searching for new restaurants to try, getting recommendations from friends, and reading reviews from other customers. Therefore, effectively using social media to promote your restaurant can make the difference between success and failure.

In this article, we will explore the importance of social media marketing for restaurants, the benefits it offers, and how to best use the main social channels to promote your restaurant.

Social media has become a powerful tool for interacting with past, present, and potential customers, sharing news and updates about your restaurant, promoting special events and offers, and creating a community of people interested in your business. Additionally, social media allows you to reach a wider audience than traditional marketing methods, enabling you to engage potential customers who might otherwise never have heard of your restaurant.

One of the most important aspects of social media marketing for restaurants is the ability to create a strong and consistent online presence that reflects your restaurant's identity and values. By creating creative and high-quality content that showcases your cuisine, atmosphere, and the experience your restaurant offers, you can highlight your uniqueness and attract potential customers' attention.

Moreover, social media allows for direct interaction with customers, answering their questions, receiving feedback and reviews, thus demonstrating your commitment to providing quality service. This type of direct interaction with customers can help build a relationship of trust and loyalty, leading to increased customer loyalty and a growing clientele.

Finally, social media marketing offers a range of analytical and monitoring tools that allow you to evaluate the effectiveness of your marketing campaigns and make necessary adjustments to optimize results. By analyzing data and statistics related to engagement, traffic, and conversions generated by your social media activities, you can gain a clear view of the return on investment and continually improve your marketing strategies.

In summary, social media marketing for restaurants is an unmissable opportunity to promote your business, create a community of loyal customers, and increase your restaurant's visibility and reputation online. In the next chapter, we will explore the main social channels used in the food industry and provide tips and strategies for making the most of them to promote your restaurant.

Main Social Channels for Restaurants

Social media offers a wide range of platforms and channels that can be used to promote a restaurant and interact with customers. Each platform has its own characteristics and specific audience, so it's important to choose the channels that best suit your target audience and marketing goals.

Below, we list the main social channels used in the food industry and provide tips on how to best use them to promote your restaurant:

- **Facebook**: With over 2 billion monthly active users, Facebook is one of the main social channels used by restaurants to promote their business. On Facebook, you can create a business page for your restaurant and share photos and videos of your dishes, special events, offers, and promotions. You can also use the review feature to let customers leave feedback about your business and respond directly to comments and questions from customers.

- **Instagram**: With over 1 billion monthly active users, Instagram is a visual platform that allows you to share photos and videos of your dishes, the atmosphere of your restaurant, and the people working in your establishment. Instagram is particularly popular among restaurants for its ability to create captivating and engaging images that can attract customers' attention and inspire them to try your dishes.

- **Twitter**: Twitter is a microblogging channel that allows you to share short messages, photos, and videos with your followers. On Twitter, you can share real-time updates about daily specials, special events, menu news, and much more. You can also use hashtags to increase the visibility of your posts and reach a wider audience.

- **LinkedIn**: LinkedIn is a professional platform that allows you to connect with other professionals in the food industry, share educational and valuable content with your audience, and build collaborative relationships with other restaurants and businesses in the sector. LinkedIn is particularly useful for networking and developing strategic partnerships that can help promote your restaurant and grow your business.

- **YouTube**: YouTube is a video-sharing platform that allows you to create tutorials, recipes, virtual tours of your restaurant, and much more. Videos are a great way to showcase your cuisine, the atmosphere of your restaurant, and the preparation of your dishes in an engaging and creative way. You can also use YouTube to interact with customers through comments and responses to questions.

- **Pinterest**: Pinterest is a visual platform that allows you to share images of your dishes, menu, decor ideas for your establishment, and much more. Pinterest is particularly useful for inspiring customers and highlighting the creativity and beauty of your dishes and restaurant.

In addition to the main social channels listed above, there are other platforms and tools that can be used to promote a restaurant, such as TikTok, Snapchat, Yelp, and TripAdvisor. It is important to analyze your restaurant's target audience and test different platforms to understand which are most effective in reaching your marketing goals.

Effective Strategies for Social Media Marketing for Restaurants

To make the best use of social media to promote your restaurant, it is important to have a clear and well-defined strategy that helps you reach your marketing goals and interact effectively with your customers. Below, we provide some effective strategies for social media marketing for restaurants:

1. **Create authentic and high-quality content**: To attract potential customers' attention and highlight your uniqueness, it is essential to create authentic, original, and high-quality content that showcases your cuisine, the atmosphere of your restaurant, and the experience offered to customers. Use captivating images and engaging videos to tell your story and show what makes your restaurant special.

2. **Engage customers through contests and giveaways**: Organizing contests and giveaways on social media is a great way to engage customers, increase your restaurant's visibility, and generate interest in your business. For example, you can ask customers to share a photo of their favorite dishes on their social pages to win a discount voucher or a free dinner at your restaurant.

3. **Respond to customer comments and reviews**: Directly interacting with customers is essential for creating a relationship of trust and loyalty that can lead

to increased clientele and positive reviews. Make sure to respond promptly to customer comments and reviews on social media, thanking them for positive feedback and professionally and courteously addressing any criticisms.

4. **Collaborate with influencers and food bloggers**: Involving influencers and food bloggers in your social media marketing can help increase your restaurant's visibility and expand your audience. Collaborate with local influencers who have a follower base similar to your target audience and ask them to try your dishes and share their experiences on social media.

5. **Plan posts and content in advance**: Planning posts and content in advance allows you to maintain a consistent and coherent presence on social media and save time and effort in managing your activities. Use scheduling tools like Hootsuite, Buffer, or Sprout Social to plan your social media posts in advance and ensure a consistent posting

frequency.

6. **Measure and monitor results**: Using social media analytics and monitoring tools helps you evaluate the effectiveness of your marketing campaigns and gain a clear view of your return on investment. Monitor key metrics such as engagement, generated traffic, conversions, and reviews to understand what works and what can be optimized to improve your results.

Social media marketing for restaurants is an extraordinary opportunity to promote your business, create a community of loyal customers, and increase your restaurant's visibility and reputation online. By effectively using the main social channels and following targeted marketing strategies, you can attract potential customers' attention, interact with existing customers, and build a trust-based relationship that can lead to increased clientele and revenue.

Remember that social media marketing is a continuous process that requires consistency, creativity, and commitment to achieve tangible results over time. Experiment with different strategies, monitor the results, and constantly adapt your strategy based on feedback and analysis to continually improve your performance and reach your marketing goals.

2. Goals to Achieve Through Social Media

Social media marketing for restaurants is a key element to increase the visibility and popularity of a venue, engaging existing customers and attracting new ones. Through an effective social media strategy, it is possible to achieve a series of goals that improve the restaurant's reputation, increase reservations, and boost overall sales.

One of the primary goals a restaurant should aim for through social media is to increase the venue's visibility. By utilizing various social channels like Facebook, Instagram, Twitter, and LinkedIn, it is possible to reach a broader audience and let users know about the restaurant's existence. Creating quality content, with captivating photos of dishes, interiors, and staff, can attract users' attention and make them interested in visiting the venue.

Additionally, an important goal is to create a

positive image of the restaurant through social media. Promptly responding to customer comments and reviews, both positive and negative, shows attentiveness to customers and a willingness to improve the service offered. Moreover, sharing success stories, special events, and exclusive promotions can help solidify the restaurant's image as a welcoming and high-quality place.

Another goal to achieve through social media is to increase customer engagement. Organizing surveys, contests, and polls on social media can encourage users to interact with the restaurant and feel part of the online community created around it. Moreover, asking customers to share their experiences through photos and reviews can create a sense of belonging and loyalty to the venue.

Social media can also be used to increase traffic to the restaurant's website and generate online reservations. Using tools like paid ads on Facebook and Instagram, it is possible to direct interested users to the restaurant's website and encourage them to book a table or catering service. Additionally, sharing promotions and special offers on social media can push users to make a reservation for dinner or an event at the venue.

Besides generating online reservations, another important goal is to increase the restaurant's overall sales through social media. Using social platforms to promote special menus, discounts, and exclusive offers can incentivize users to visit the venue and spend more. Additionally, creating partnerships with influencers and collaborations with other restaurants or brands can increase the venue's exposure and attract new interested customers.

Finally, a long-term goal to achieve through social media is to build a loyal and devoted customer base for the restaurant. Consistently communicating with customers through social media, offering interesting and engaging content, can help create an emotional connection with the venue and foster customer loyalty. Additionally, organizing exclusive events and offering special benefits to the most loyal customers can encourage them to stay and frequently return to the restaurant.

Through an effective social media marketing strategy, restaurants can achieve a series of goals that increase visibility, improve image, engage customers, generate online reservations, boost sales, and build a loyal customer base. By using social channels smartly and creatively, it is possible to fully exploit the potential of social media to promote the restaurant and achieve tangible results in the short and long term.

3.Creating a Social Media Profile

In recent years, social media has become an indispensable tool for the promotion and marketing of any business, especially restaurants. Creating a profile on platforms like Facebook, Instagram, and Twitter can help restaurateurs reach a wider audience and maintain a constant relationship with customers. In this article, we will examine the steps to create an effective social media profile for a restaurant, as well as some marketing strategies that can be used to promote the business and attract customers.

Step 1: Choosing the Platforms

The first decision to make is which social platforms to create a profile for the restaurant on. The most common and widely used platforms in the restaurant industry are Facebook, Instagram, and Twitter, but there are also other platforms like Pinterest, Snapchat, and TikTok that might be useful in certain contexts.

Facebook is the most widely used social platform in the world and offers many opportunities for promoting a restaurant. You can create a business page on Facebook where you can share content, promote events, and interact with customers. Instagram is an image-centric social network and can be particularly useful for sharing photos of the restaurant's dishes and showcasing the appealing look of the venue. Twitter is a more streamlined and fast-paced platform, ideal for sharing last-minute news, updates on opening hours, and special promotions.

Once you have chosen the platforms to use, it is important to create consistent and recognizable profiles for your restaurant. It is advisable to use the same logo and graphics across all platforms so that customers can easily identify your restaurant's presence on social media.

Step 2: Creating the Profile

Once you have chosen the platforms to use, it is time to create the restaurant's profile. Each platform has specific procedures to follow for creating a business profile. For example, on Facebook, you need to create a business page and fill in all the information about the restaurant, such as the address, opening hours, contact information, and a brief description of the business.

On Instagram, you can create a business profile linked to an existing Facebook page, making it easy to share content between the two platforms. It is important to include a catchy bio that briefly describes the restaurant and includes a direct link to the website or online menu if available.

On Twitter, you can create a business account that shares quick updates and news about the restaurant. It is useful to include a brief description of the restaurant in the profile header, along with an eye-catching photo of the venue or a dish from the menu.

Step 3: Creating Content

Once the restaurant's profile is created, it is time to start sharing interesting and engaging content to attract customers' attention. It is important to create a content strategy that is consistent with the restaurant's image and style and that takes into account the target clientele.

On Facebook, you can share photos of menu dishes, behind-the-scenes videos from the kitchen, and special promotions for customers. You can also create Facebook events to promote themed dinners or special evenings and invite customers to participate.

On Instagram, you can maximize the power of images with captivating photos of the restaurant's dishes, venue, and staff. It is important to use relevant hashtags and tag the restaurant's location to increase the visibility of your photos.

On X (formerly Twitter), you can share quick updates on ongoing events, opening hours, and restaurant promotions. It is useful to engage customers with polls, games, or questions to stimulate interaction and increase engagement.

Step 4: Interacting with Customers

A fundamental aspect of social media marketing for restaurants is constant interaction with customers. It is important to respond promptly to customer comments and reviews, both positive and negative, to show attentiveness and care for your clientele.

On Facebook, you can respond to comments directly on the business page and send private messages to customers to resolve any issues or requests. It is important to be available and friendly with customers to create a relationship of mutual trust.

On Instagram, you can respond to comments under your photos and interact with customers through stories. It is useful to use direct message functions to answer customers' questions more quickly and directly.

On X, you can respond to customers' tweets and interact with them via direct messages. It is important to be available to resolve any issues or doubts customers may have to maintain a positive online reputation.

Step 5: Marketing Strategies

In addition to creating content and interacting with customers, there are some marketing strategies that can be used to promote a restaurant on social media. One of the most effective strategies is to collaborate with influencers or food bloggers who have a large number of followers and an audience interested in dining out.

Food bloggers can share positive reviews of your restaurant, photos of menu dishes, and promote special events or promotions. It is important to select influencers who align with your restaurant's image and style to maximize the impact of the collaborations.

Another effective strategy is to create contests and giveaways on social media to engage customers and attract new followers. For example, you can organize a photo contest where customers are invited to share a photo of their favorite dishes from the restaurant with a specific hashtag to win a special prize.

Additionally, you can promote special events like themed dinners, musical evenings, or guided tastings through social media to attract customers and increase your restaurant's visibility.

Conclusions

Creating a social media profile for a restaurant can be an effective way to promote the business, attract customers, and maintain a constant relationship with your clientele. It is important to create interesting and engaging content, interact with customers promptly, and show attentiveness and care towards them.

By using the right tools and strategies, you can fully exploit the potential of social media to increase your restaurant's visibility, generate new customers, and retain existing ones. With a well-structured social media marketing strategy that aligns with your restaurant's image, you can achieve significant results and solidify your online presence in the restaurant industry.

4. Profile Optimization

Profile optimization on social media is crucial for every business, especially for restaurants aiming to promote their establishment and attract new customers. In this text, we will delve into the importance of optimizing the profile name, profile picture, description, and website link on platforms like Facebook, Instagram, X, and LinkedIn.

1. Profile Name: The profile name on social media is the first thing customers see when they visit the restaurant's page. It is important to choose a name that is easily recognizable and consistent with the restaurant's name. Additionally, including useful information such as the type of cuisine offered, location, and any specialties can be beneficial.

For example, if the restaurant is named "La Pizzeria del Centro," the profile name could be "La Pizzeria del Centro - Neapolitan Pizza in Pavia." This immediately gives potential customers a clear idea of what the establishment offers and its location.

2. Profile Picture: The profile picture is a fundamental visual element for the restaurant's social media profile. It is recommended to use the restaurant's logo as the profile picture to make the brand immediately recognizable.

If the restaurant doesn't have a logo, you can use a high-quality photo of the entrance or one of the most famous dishes offered. However, it's crucial that the chosen image is of high quality and reflects the style and atmosphere of the restaurant.

3. Profile Description: The profile description is the ideal place to provide detailed information about the restaurant, its history, specialties offered, and the establishment's philosophy. It is also advisable to include practical information such as opening hours, phone number for reservations, and links to delivery platforms or the website.

Example of a profile description for a restaurant: "Welcome to La Pizzeria del Centro, the perfect place to enjoy authentic Neapolitan pizzas in Pavia! Visit us daily from 6:00 PM to 11:00 PM and book your table by calling XXXXXXXXXX. Follow us to stay updated on our news and promotions!"

4. Website Link: Including the link to the restaurant's website is essential for guiding interested customers to further information about the venue, viewing the complete menu, booking a table, or placing an online order. If the restaurant doesn't have a website, you can insert a link to the Facebook or Instagram page of the establishment.

Example of a post on Facebook: "Discover our brand new autumn menu on our website and book your table for an unforgettable dinner! www.lapizzeriadellecentro.it"

Conclusion

Optimizing the profile on social media for restaurants is a fundamental operation to attract new customers, promote the business, and create a strong online presence. By following these tips and carefully managing every detail of the profile, the restaurant can stand out from the competition and build a community of loyal and passionate customers.

5.Content Creation - Types of Content to Share (Food Photos, Menu, Special Events, Offers)

Creating compelling and high-quality content is crucial for attracting and engaging customers on social media, especially in the restaurant industry. There are various types of content that a restaurant can share to promote its business and intrigue potential customers.

One of the most effective types of content for restaurants is food photos. Images showcasing creatively prepared dishes and presented in an appealing manner are highly engaging for audiences. Photos of popular dishes and daily specials can whet appetites and motivate people to visit the restaurant to try them out. It's important to ensure that the images are of high quality, bright, clear, and well-composed. Additionally, using filters and visual effects can further enhance the attractiveness of the photos.

In addition to food photos, a restaurant can also share its menu on social media. Displaying available dishes and their prices can help familiarize the audience with the culinary offerings of the establishment and assist customers in deciding what to order before they arrive. You can create posts dedicated to individual dishes or showcase complete menu proposals for special occasions such as Valentine's Day, Easter, Christmas, or New Year's Eve. This approach can build anticipation and pique customer interest in visiting the restaurant for specific events.

Another important type of content to share is special events organized by the restaurant. These could include themed dinners, tastings, live music nights, karaoke nights, stand-up comedy nights, or any event that can attract and engage customers. Publicizing these events on social media is essential for ensuring their success and maximizing participation. You can create dedicated posts for events, share promotional videos, post trailers on Instagram Stories, create events on

Facebook, and encourage followers to share the information with their friends and family.

Furthermore, restaurants can use their social media pages to share special offers and promotions. For example, you can create posts dedicated to discounts, coupons, fixed-price special menus, happy hour deals, promotions for special occasions like birthdays or graduations. These posts can be an effective way to attract new customers, reward the loyalty of existing ones, and increase restaurant sales. It's important for offers to be clear, enticing, and have an expiration date to create a sense of urgency among customers.

In addition to the aforementioned content types, there are other content creation strategies that restaurants can adopt to promote their business on social media. For instance, you can create behind-the-scenes videos showcasing the kitchen operations, the dish preparation process, staff interactions with customers. These videos can be highly engaging and allow customers to feel involved in the restaurant's daily life. Moreover, restaurants can share reviews and testimonials from satisfied customers to showcase public appreciation and encourage others to experience the culinary offerings of the venue.

Finally, it's important to stay abreast of current trends and what works best on social media. For example, video content sharing is increasingly popular, so restaurants should consider creating original videos, recipe tutorials, chef interviews, live cooking sessions, or daily special presentation videos. Additionally, interacting with the audience through comments, direct messages, and polls fosters deeper engagement and creates an active and loyal online community.

Creating original, compelling, and high-quality content is fundamental to the success of a restaurant on social media. Sharing food photos, menus, special events, offers, behind-the-scenes videos, and customer reviews can help promote the business, attract new customers, reward the loyalty of existing ones, and create an active and engaged online community. It's important to experiment with different types of content, monitor performance, and adjust social media marketing strategies based on results to ensure long-term success and business growth.

6. Use of Hashtags and Geotags to Increase Visibility

In recent years, using hashtags and geotags on social media has become essential for restaurants aiming to boost their online visibility. Through these simple social media marketing strategies, it's possible to reach a wider audience, attract new customers, and retain existing ones. In this article, we will explore how to effectively utilize hashtags and geotags to promote a restaurant and enhance its presence on social media.

Firstly, it's important to understand what hashtags and geotags are and how they function. Hashtags are words or phrases preceded by the symbol # that are used to categorize content on social media. For instance, if a restaurant posts a photo of a pasta dish, it might use hashtags like #pasta #italianfood #foodie to make the post more discoverable by people interested in those topics. Geotags, on the other hand, provide geographic location information from where a content is posted on social media. By using geotags, a restaurant can pinpoint its exact location and make it visible to users searching for venues in the area.

Strategically using hashtags and geotags can yield several benefits for a restaurant. Firstly, it allows reaching a broader audience interested in the restaurant's offerings. With hashtags, restaurant posts can be seen by users following those specific themes or searching for related content. Geotags help attract local customers who are in the vicinity of the restaurant and may be interested in visiting. Moreover, using hashtags and geotags can enhance the restaurant's visibility on search engines and increase traffic to its social media profile.

To maximize the effectiveness of hashtags and geotags, it's crucial to choose them strategically and accurately. Hashtags should be relevant to the content being posted and the industry in which the restaurant operates. For example, an Italian restaurant might use hashtags like #pizza #pasta #italianrestaurant to categorize its posts under topics related to Italian cuisine. It's also advisable to avoid overly generic or extremely popular hashtags, as the post could easily get lost among similar content. Opting for more specific and targeted hashtags helps attract a more qualified and interested audience.

Geotags should be used accurately to pinpoint the restaurant's exact location. This is particularly useful for venues aiming to attract customers in their vicinity and promote local events or special offers targeted at residents. Additionally, some social media platforms like Instagram offer the option to create a custom geolocation for the restaurant, which can be a great strategy to enhance online visibility.

In addition to using hashtags and geotags in posts, restaurants can leverage these strategies in other situations to increase their visibility on social media. For example, using hashtags in comments or replies to followers can make content more discoverable. Moreover, creating custom hashtags for special events or restaurant promotional campaigns actively engages customers and promotes word-of-mouth online.

Another effective way to use hashtags and geotags to promote a restaurant is by participating in contests or collaborating with industry influencers. Organizing a social media contest with a dedicated hashtag can increase customer interaction and attract new followers interested in the restaurant. Collaborating with influencers allows reaching a broader and more qualified audience who may be interested in trying the restaurant's dishes and sharing them on their social media profiles.

Finally, it's important to monitor the effectiveness of hashtags and geotags used to promote the restaurant and make adjustments based on results. Using social media analytics tools can help evaluate the performance of marketing strategies and identify strengths and weaknesses. For instance, it's possible to track how many users interacted with a specific hashtag or geotag and measure increases in followers or traffic to the social media profile.

Using hashtags and geotags on social media can be an excellent marketing strategy to increase a restaurant's visibility and attract new customers. Through these simple techniques, it's possible to reach a broader and more qualified audience, improve online presence, and boost traffic to the restaurant's social media profile. With proper planning and ongoing monitoring of results, hashtags and geotags can become powerful allies in promoting a restaurant and introducing it to an increasingly broader and food-loving audience.

7.User Engagement - Responding to Comments and Messages

User engagement on social media is crucial for any business, especially for restaurants. Managing a restaurant's online presence requires not only posting high-quality and appealing content but also effectively interacting with followers.

Responding to comments and messages is a crucial aspect of social media marketing for restaurants as it allows for building a deeper relationship with customers and maintaining interaction between followers and the brand. In this article, we will examine the importance of responding to comments and messages on social media for restaurants, along with practical tips on how to do it effectively.

Firstly, it's important to understand why responding to comments and messages is so important for restaurants. Firstly, responding to comments demonstrates care and attention towards customers, making them feel that their feedback is heard and appreciated. In a competitive industry like dining, maintaining a positive relationship with customers can make the difference between success and failure.

Moreover, responding to comments and messages allows for creating a genuine dialogue with followers, which can increase engagement and customer loyalty towards the restaurant. Apart from providing useful information and resolving any issues, responding to comments can also be an opportunity to subtly and effectively promote products and services.

Lastly, responding to comments and messages on social media is also important for managing the restaurant's online reputation. Leaving a negative comment or review unanswered can have a very negative impact on potential customers' perception of the brand, while a timely and professional response can turn a negative experience into an opportunity to improve and show openness and transparency.

That said, responding to comments and messages on social media for restaurants can be challenging, especially considering the volume of interactions that can accumulate on platforms like Facebook, Instagram, and Twitter. Here are some practical tips for effectively managing interactions with followers and creating a positive online experience for customers:

1. **Be Prompt in Responses:** In today's information age, consumers expect quick and immediate responses from businesses, especially on social media. Aim to respond to comments and messages within a few hours of posting to demonstrate attention and interest in your followers.

2. **Personalize Responses:** Avoid standardized responses and personalize your replies based on the received comment or

message. Show empathy and understanding towards the needs and concerns of your customers. Responding in a personalized manner can make a difference in creating an authentic and lasting relationship with your followers.

3. **Maintain a Professional Tone:** Even when faced with a negative or critical comment, avoid responding with argumentative or aggressive tones. Maintain a calm and professional attitude and aim to resolve any issues courteously and respectfully to avoid worsening the situation and damaging the restaurant's reputation.

4. **Be Creative and Proactive:** In addition to reactive responses, actively participate in online conversations and stimulate engagement among your followers. Organize contests, polls, and social initiatives to engage customers and encourage participation in the restaurant's online community.

5. **Monitor Interactions Constantly:**
Consistently monitor interactions on social media and strategically respond to reviews. In addition to comments and direct messages, it's also important to monitor customer reviews on platforms like TripAdvisor, Google Maps, and Yelp. Respond appropriately to both negative and positive reviews to demonstrate transparency and commitment to improving customer experience.

Responding to comments and messages on social media is a fundamental aspect of social media marketing for restaurants, enabling a closer bond with customers and effective management of the brand's online reputation. By following the practical tips provided in this article and dedicating resources and attention to managing online interactions, restaurants can create a strong and positive online presence that can lead to increased customer loyalty and business growth.

8.Collaborations with Influencers and Bloggers

In recent years, social media marketing has proven to be a powerful tool to help restaurants promote their business and increase online visibility. Particularly, collaborations with influencers and bloggers have become increasingly popular as they allow reaching a broader audience and generating more interest around the restaurant.

To identify the most suitable influencers and bloggers for your restaurant, it is important to consider several aspects such as the target audience, the type of cuisine offered, geographical location, available budget, and the brand image you want to convey. Below, we will analyze some of the key steps to follow in identifying the right influencers and bloggers to collaborate with your restaurant.

Firstly, conducting thorough research on social media is essential to identify influencers and bloggers who are active in the food sector and have a significant following. There are various online tools available to monitor the online presence of these individuals and evaluate their authority and the effectiveness of their posts.

Once potential collaborators are identified, it is crucial to carefully evaluate their profile and communication style to determine if they align with the image and values of your restaurant. For instance, if your restaurant specializes in gourmet cuisine, it might be appropriate to collaborate with influencers who have an audience interested in fine dining and sophistication. Conversely, if your restaurant offers a more casual menu or street food, it may be more suitable to seek influencers with a younger and dynamic appeal.

Another factor to consider is the location of influencers and bloggers. If your restaurant is situated in a specific city or region, collaborating with individuals who have a significant following in that area can be advantageous to reach a closer and potentially interested audience.

Once the most suitable influencers and bloggers for your restaurant are identified, it is important to establish contact with them and propose a collaboration. It is advisable to clearly and comprehensively present the offer and the benefits that the restaurant can provide in exchange for collaboration, such as invitations to special lunches or dinners, meal discounts, giveaways, or personalized gifts.

Furthermore, planning a carefully crafted communication and marketing strategy during the collaboration with influencers and bloggers is crucial to maximize the impact of their posts and generate greater engagement from the audience. For example, you can organize special events or exclusive tastings for influencers, involve them in the creation of new dishes or menus, and offer them exclusive content to share on their channels.

Creating collaborations to increase the visibility of the restaurant is an excellent strategy to attract more customers and enhance the reputation of the establishment. Collaborations can be established with various entities such as bloggers, influencers, associations, or other restaurants, and are essential for attracting new customers and retaining existing ones.

One of the first steps to take in creating effective collaborations is to identify key players in the restaurant and food & beverage sector, both locally and nationally. You can start by contacting bloggers and influencers who share content related to food and gastronomy, proposing a possible collaboration that can bring mutual benefits.

Collaborations can take various forms; for example, a food blogger could organize a tasting day at the restaurant and then share their impressions and photos of the experience on their social media channels. Alternatively, you could organize a special event in collaboration with an industry association, inviting your customers to participate and taste special dishes prepared for the occasion.

Another way to increase the visibility of the restaurant is to establish partnerships with other restaurants in the area, such as organizing joint dinners or collaborating to promote culinary events. This can help expand your network and increase the visibility of your restaurant, reaching new potential customers.

Another effective strategy to increase the visibility of the restaurant is to use customer reviews and feedback on various social media channels and online review platforms. This allows you to show users the satisfaction of past customers and encourage them to try your establishment. It is important to respond to all reviews, both positive and negative, demonstrating attention and interest in customer opinions.

To increase the visibility of the restaurant, it is also essential to create an effective social media marketing strategy, including the consistent publication of high-quality content, management of paid advertisements, and collaboration with influencers and bloggers in the industry. Maintaining consistency in the tone and style of published content is important, showing the personality of the restaurant and engaging followers with interesting and original content.

Furthermore, it is crucial to make the most of platforms like Instagram, Facebook, YouTube, and TikTok by creating captivating and engaging visual content that can attract the attention of potential customers. For example, you can post photos and videos of your most delicious dishes, behind-the-scenes moments in the kitchen, or special events organized at the restaurant.

Another effective strategy to increase the visibility of the restaurant is to collaborate with complementary brands or companies that can promote your establishment through partnerships or sponsorships. For example, you could organize a tasting evening in collaboration with a local wine company or a themed dinner with a high-quality gastronomic products brand.

Finally, to increase the visibility of the restaurant, it is important to take care of your online presence, ensuring that the website is up-to-date and optimized for search engines, and that contact information and reviews are easily accessible. Moreover, it is crucial to constantly monitor the performance of marketing campaigns and collaborations, evaluating the results obtained and making any necessary corrections and improvements.

Creating collaborations to increase the visibility of the restaurant is an effective and advantageous strategy to attract new customers, improve the reputation of the establishment, and establish lasting partnerships in the restaurant sector. It is important to identify key players in the sector and create synergies that can bring mutual benefits, making the most of the potential of social media and online platforms to reach an increasingly large and attentive audience.

Finally, it is essential to constantly monitor the results of collaborations with influencers and bloggers, evaluating the effectiveness of the actions taken and making any necessary corrections or improvements. It is important to measure metrics such as the number of views, likes, and comments received, shares, and new followers acquired, to understand if the collaboration has achieved the desired results and if it has been in line with the set objectives.

9.How to Advertise: Pay-Per-Click and Pay-Per-Thousand Views

Social media marketing has become a crucial tool for promoting a business, especially in the restaurant sector. In particular, restaurants can greatly benefit from targeted advertising strategies on social media, which efficiently reach a wide audience of potential customers. Among the various options available for online advertising, one of the most common are pay-per-click (PPC) and pay-per-thousand views (PPM), two payment models that offer different advantages and customization possibilities to suit the specific needs of each activity to be done on popular social networks such as Instagram, Facebook, and TikTok.

Pay-per-click is an online advertising model where the advertiser pays only when a user clicks on the ad, thus directing traffic to their website or social media page. This model allows for precise monitoring of the effectiveness of advertising campaigns, as there is a clear idea of the return on investment (ROI) based on the number of clicks received. Additionally, PPC allows setting daily or total budgets, ensuring total control over advertising expenses and the distribution of ads.

On the other hand, pay-per-thousand views is an online advertising model where the advertiser pays a fixed rate for every thousand ad views. This model is particularly suitable for branding and broad visibility campaigns, as it allows reaching a large and diversified audience without necessarily generating direct interactions with the ad. Similarly, it is possible to set a precise budget and establish visibility goals to measure the effectiveness of the campaign.

For restaurants looking to promote their business on social media, both pay-per-click and pay-per-thousand views offer advantages and customization possibilities that can be leveraged according to objectives and available resources. Below, we will explore some practical strategies and tips to make the most of these two online advertising models within the context of social media marketing for restaurants.

Pay-Per-Click Strategies for Restaurants

1. **Precise Targeting:** One of the main features of pay-per-click is the ability to precisely select the target audience for your advertising campaign. For restaurants, it's crucial to identify customer segments most likely to visit the establishment, such as local residents, enthusiasts of ethnic cuisine, or those interested in specific types of dishes. By using advanced targeting tools like demographic and behavioral options offered by social media platforms, it is possible to reach exactly the people you want to engage.

2. **Creativity and Originality:** To capture users' attention and stand out from the competition, it's important to create creative and original advertising. For restaurants, this can include eye-catching images of menu

items, behind-the-scenes kitchen videos, or compelling stories about culinary traditions from the region. The use of high-quality visual content is essential to spark interest and stimulate the appetite of potential customers.

3. **Effective Call-to-Action:** To ensure that an advertisement leads to conversions, such as table reservations or online orders, it's important to include clear and persuasive call-to-action (CTA) phrases. For example, phrases like "Book Now," "Explore Our Menu," or "Order Online" can guide users to take the desired action. Testing different types of CTAs is advisable to identify the most effective ones for your target audience.

4. **Monitoring and Optimization:** To maximize the effectiveness of pay-per-click campaigns, it's crucial to constantly monitor ad performance and make optimizations based on results. Through analytics and conversion tracking tools, it is possible to measure the effectiveness of various campaigns, identify strengths and weaknesses, and make timely

corrections to improve return on investment. Continuous iteration is essential for optimizing campaigns and maximizing performance.

5. **Integration with Online Booking Tools:** For restaurants offering online booking services, integrating pay-per-click ads with booking tools available on the website or social media can direct interested users straight to the booking page. This facilitates the booking process and increases the chances of conversion. Integration with online booking systems also allows for accurate monitoring of the impact of advertising campaigns on the number of bookings made.

Pay-Per-Thousand Views Strategies for Restaurants

1. **Brand Awareness:** Pay-per-thousand views is particularly effective for increasing brand visibility and awareness among a broad

and diverse audience. For restaurants aiming to attract local and international clientele, investing in brand awareness campaigns that highlight the values, history, and quality of the cuisine is important. Using eye-catching visuals, memorable slogans, and engaging stories can help create a positive image of the restaurant in consumers' minds.

2. **Sponsorships and Collaborations:** To expand the reach of pay-per-thousand views campaigns, restaurants can consider sponsorships and collaborations with influencers, bloggers, or industry media. Associating with prominent figures in the restaurant or gastronomy world can enhance the credibility and attractiveness of the brand, making a positive impact on online advertising campaigns. Strategic collaborations can help expand the fan and follower base of the restaurant, increasing visibility and reputation.

3. **Engaging and Viral Content:** To maximize the impact of pay-per-thousand

views campaigns, creating engaging and viral content that sparks interest and sharing among users is important. For example, creating recipe tutorial videos, gastronomy-focused contests, or interviews with famous chefs can be effective. Creating original and engaging content is crucial for capturing audience attention and encouraging sharing on social media, thereby amplifying brand visibility and restaurant offerings.

4. **Native Advertising and Sponsored Content:** Another effective strategy to make the most of the pay-per-thousand views model is to invest in native advertising and sponsored content, which seamlessly integrates within social media platforms without appearing intrusive or disruptive. For example, creating sponsored articles on food blogs, reviews of dishes on industry podcasts, or cooking tutorial videos on video platforms like YouTube. Native advertising allows reaching the audience in a non-intrusive way, increasing interest and user engagement.

5. **Analysis and Reporting:** To evaluate the effectiveness of pay-per-thousand views campaigns, it's important to constantly monitor ad performance and analyze visibility and engagement data generated. Through views and interaction analytics tools, it is possible to measure campaign effectiveness, identify the most appreciated content by the audience, and pinpoint the most profitable traffic sources. Data analysis allows for optimizing ongoing campaigns and planning more effective strategies in the future to maximize advertising investment returns.

In conclusion, pay-per-click and pay-per-thousand views are two online advertising models that offer businesses a range of advantages and customization options to promote their products and services on social media. For restaurants operating in a highly competitive and ever-changing sector, adopting targeted and effective advertising strategies to reach and engage their target audience is crucial. By leveraging the potential offered by pay-per-click and pay-per-thousand views, restaurants can increase brand visibility, attract new customers, and boost sales, contributing to the success and growth of the business.

10. Performance Monitoring

Performance monitoring is a crucial activity for any marketing endeavor, especially within the realm of social media marketing for restaurants. In such a competitive and constantly evolving landscape, having accurate and up-to-date data is essential for evaluating the effectiveness of strategies and making informed decisions to optimize outcomes.

One of the most widely used tools for monitoring social media performance in the restaurant sector is Google Analytics. This free tool provides a wide range of metrics and reports that allow tracking user interactions with the restaurant's website and social profiles. For instance, it enables monitoring metrics such as unique visitors, average time spent on site, most visited pages, and conversion events like table reservations or online orders.

In addition to Google Analytics, there are numerous specialized tools for social media monitoring, such as Hootsuite, Sprout Social, Buffer, and Brandwatch. These tools facilitate efficient management of multiple social accounts, post scheduling, user interaction monitoring, demographic and geographic data analysis, engagement measurement, and identification of trends and publishing opportunities.

One of the most important indicators to monitor in social media marketing for restaurants is engagement, which refers to user interaction with content posted on social platforms. This can be measured through metrics like likes, comments, shares, and profile visits. High engagement rates signal audience interest and appreciation, contributing to improved visibility and reputation of the restaurant on social media.

Another key metric to monitor is reach, which denotes the number of people exposed to the restaurant's content on social media. A broader reach translates to increased visibility and the potential to reach a wider audience, thereby enhancing the likelihood of generating leads and conversions. It's crucial to monitor both organic reach, obtained naturally, and paid reach, achieved through advertising campaigns.

Furthermore, monitoring the quality of published content and user interaction with it is essential. For example, analyzing which types of posts generate more engagement, determining optimal posting times, identifying effective hashtags, and understanding themes that resonate most with the audience. Such insights can be instrumental in optimizing content strategy and maximizing results.

Performance monitoring in social media for restaurants goes beyond quantity of interactions and views; it also involves assessing the quality of generated contacts and their conversion potential. Identifying active and loyal followers—those who regularly interact with content and demonstrate genuine interest in the restaurant—is important for fostering deeper and lasting relationships.

In addition to numerical and quantitative data, it's beneficial to monitor the restaurant's online reputation, including user opinions and feedback on social media and review platforms like TripAdvisor and Yelp. Responding promptly to both positive and negative comments, managing reviews professionally and constructively, and using feedback to enhance services are crucial aspects.

Lastly, performance monitoring in social media for restaurants should be a continuous and dynamic process. Constantly testing new strategies, analyzing results, and making necessary adjustments and optimizations are essential. The ability to quickly adapt to new trends and consumer needs is fundamental to maintaining competitiveness in the sector and driving social media success for the restaurant.

Performance monitoring is a pivotal element in social media marketing for restaurants, enabling evaluation of strategy effectiveness, identification of growth opportunities, and maintenance of a strong and lasting relationship with the target audience. Leveraging advanced analytics tools and understanding key performance indicators are essential for achieving tangible results and enhancing the restaurant's brand on social media.

11. Evaluating the Effectiveness of Adopted Strategies and Making Necessary Adjustments

In recent years, social media marketing has become an indispensable tool for businesses aiming to effectively and specifically promote their products and services. In the restaurant sector, in particular, social media has emerged as a preferred channel to reach potential customers, foster existing client loyalty, and communicate quickly and directly.

Within a restaurant context, social media marketing serves various purposes: promoting menu dishes, advertising special events, sharing customer reviews and testimonials, offering promotions and discounts, and much more. However, achieving concrete results hinges on adopting effective strategies and continually monitoring outcomes to make necessary adjustments and optimizations.

To evaluate the effectiveness of strategies

adopted in social media marketing for a restaurant, it's crucial to analyze several key factors, including:

1. **Objectives:** Clearly defining marketing goals that social media efforts aim to achieve —such as increasing customer base, boosting reservations, promoting new dishes or events, etc. Only with clear objectives can one assess if adopted strategies are yielding desired outcomes.

2. **Audience:** Deeply understanding the restaurant's target audience to create tailored content that resonates with them. Monitoring follower trends across social channels helps gain insights into the most interested and active customers.

3. **Content:** The quality of content shared on social media is pivotal in capturing audience attention and interest. Thus, it's important to post high-quality photos of menu items, share recipes, promote special events,

etc. Monitoring engagement metrics (likes, comments, shares) helps understand which content types perform best with the audience.

4. **Frequency:** Maintaining a consistent and active social media presence by regularly sharing content is important. Too few posts might diminish audience interest, while too many could be perceived as intrusive. Hence, finding a balance and monitoring how posting frequency impacts results is essential.

5. **Interaction:** One of social media's key features is its ability to directly interact with customers. Therefore, promptly responding to follower comments and questions demonstrates interest and attentiveness. Monitoring audience interaction helps gauge whether adopted strategies are generating engagement and involvement.

Once these aspects are evaluated, it becomes possible to determine if adopted strategies are delivering desired results or if adjustments are needed to enhance social media communication effectiveness. Suggestions for making necessary adjustments may include:

1. **Analyzing Results:** Utilizing analytics tools to monitor performance across social channels, tracking engagement metrics, follower growth, website traffic, and reservations. Concrete data informs whether adopted strategies are effective or require intervention.

2. **Testing New Strategies:** Experimenting with new content types, posting times, post formats, etc., to identify alternative strategies that may generate better audience engagement and interest.

3. **Involving the Team:** Engaging the restaurant team in social media management, seeking suggestions and feedback on content to share, events to promote, etc. Involving the entire team can lead to fresh and original ideas for improving social media communication.

4. **Collaborating with Influencers:**
Partnering with influencers or bloggers in the
food and lifestyle sector to promote the
restaurant can effectively expand visibility
and reach new potential customers.
Monitoring the impact of influencer
collaborations helps gauge the effectiveness of
such investments.

5. **Monitoring Competition:** Analyzing
social media strategies employed by
competitors can provide insights into what
works and what doesn't in the restaurant
sector. Subscribing to competitor newsletters,
following their social channels, and analyzing
customer reviews helps identify new
improvement opportunities.

Evaluating the effectiveness of social media
marketing strategies for a restaurant is an
ongoing and evolving process that requires
continuous monitoring, data analysis, and
adaptability to changing market demands.
Making necessary adjustments based on

achieved results is crucial for ensuring social media communication success and achieving marketing objectives.

12. Review Management

Managing online reviews is crucial for any business, whether it's a restaurant, hotel, retail store, or any service-oriented establishment. Customer reviews are a powerful marketing tool that can significantly influence potential customers' purchasing decisions.

Reviews can be positive or negative, and it's essential to handle them correctly to maximize the benefits they can bring. Responding to positive reviews is important as it shows appreciation and gratitude for customers' positive feedback. Additionally, a personalized and thoughtful response can strengthen the customer relationship and make them feel valued. For example, if a customer leaves a positive review on TripAdvisor praising the restaurant's food and excellent service, the restaurant manager could respond by thanking the customer for their feedback and inviting them to visit again soon.

On the other hand, negative reviews should be handled with equal care, if not more. It's important to remember that a negative review not only has the potential to damage the business's reputation but can also provide valuable insights into areas needing improvement. Responding calmly and professionally to a negative review is essential for managing the situation effectively. It's important to demonstrate to the dissatisfied customer that their opinion is valued and that efforts will be made to resolve the issue. For instance, if a customer leaves a negative review on TripAdvisor complaining about poor service at the restaurant, the manager could respond by apologizing for the experience and offering a resolution such as a voucher or discount for a future visit.

However, reviews aren't just about managing an activity's online reputation. They can also be a valuable tool for improving the services offered. Many review sites like TripAdvisor offer the ability to analyze review data to identify strengths and weaknesses in the business. For example, a restaurant might notice that many reviews complain about excessively long wait times or rude service. Using this information, the restaurant could decide to implement a new reservation system or organize staff training.

Furthermore, positive reviews can be used for marketing purposes. Displaying customer testimonials on the business's website or social media can help build trust with potential customers and encourage them to book or visit the business. Collaborating with influencers or bloggers who write positive reviews on TripAdvisor or other review sites can also be an excellent social media marketing strategy to increase the business's visibility.

Ultimately, managing online reviews is an ongoing process that requires care, attention, and dedication. Responding appropriately to reviews, using feedback to improve services, and leveraging positive reviews for marketing purposes are just some of the strategies that can help maximize the benefits of online reviews. With the right focus and commitment, customer reviews can become a valuable ally in growing and enhancing a business.

13.Following New Social Media Trends and Adapting Your Strategy Accordingly

In recent years, social media has become an essential tool for promoting and increasing visibility for any business, including restaurants. Following new social media trends and adapting your strategy accordingly is crucial to ensure the success of a venue in an increasingly competitive and evolving market.

Social media marketing for restaurants encompasses not only promoting dishes and services offered but also building a strong and consistent brand image, engaging with customers, and creating an online community. In a world where people spend more time on social media platforms like Facebook, Instagram, Twitter, and TikTok, it's important for restaurants to be present and active.

To follow new social media trends and adapt your strategy accordingly, it's important to keep an eye on updates and innovations from the most popular platforms. For instance, Instagram has emerged as one of the most used platforms for restaurant promotion, owing to its visual nature and the ability to share photos and videos of menu offerings.

One of the latest trends on Instagram is the use of Stories, which are content pieces that last only 24 hours and allow restaurants to share behind-the-scenes moments, special offers, and previews of new dishes. Moreover, Instagram has introduced the ability to make reservations directly from the platform, making it easier for customers to book a table at the restaurant.

Another significant trend on social media is leveraging influencers to promote restaurants. Influencers are individuals with large online followings who can help increase a restaurant's visibility and attract new customers. Collaborating with local or national influencers can be an excellent way to introduce your venue to a broader and more diverse audience.

Additionally, it's important to monitor current social media trends and adjust your strategy accordingly. For example, in recent years, vegan and vegetarian food options have gained significant traction on social media, with more people interested in discovering new dishes and restaurants offering cruelty-free options. Adapting the restaurant's menu to cater to vegan and vegetarian customers and promoting veg-friendly options on social media can help attract a wider and sustainability-conscious audience.

Beyond current trends, it's also crucial to monitor the performance of your social media marketing campaigns and adjust your strategy accordingly. Using analytics tools like Google Analytics or Facebook and Instagram Insights can help understand which content performs best, which platforms are most effective, and who your restaurant's target audience is.

For example, if promotional posts show low engagement rates, you might consider shifting towards a content marketing strategy with original and informative content that resonates with your audience. If most of your customers are coming from Facebook, you might focus your social media marketing efforts on that platform and test new strategies to increase restaurant visibility.

Ultimately, it's important to be flexible and ready to adapt your strategy based on market demands and customer feedback. The social media landscape is constantly evolving, and what worked well even a few years ago may not be as effective today. Continuously monitoring the performance of social media marketing campaigns, testing new strategies and approaches can help stay competitive and maintain a relevant and engaging online presence for customers.

Following new social media trends and adapting your strategy accordingly is essential for ensuring a restaurant's success in the increasingly competitive landscape of social media marketing. Keeping up with updates from major platforms, collaborating with influencers, adapting the menu to meet customer needs, and continually monitoring campaign performance are just a few steps restaurants can take to remain relevant and competitive on social media.

14. Storytelling for Restaurants

In the digital era we live in, social media marketing has become essential for any business, including restaurants. But how can we harness the power of storytelling to effectively promote our restaurants on social media?

Talking about food and restaurants offers many storytelling opportunities. It's about food, innovation, tradition, emotions, and experiences. Restaurants can tell stories that engage their customers, excite them, and convince them to experience the pleasure of dining at their establishment.

One of the most effective techniques for creating storytelling for a restaurant on social media is to showcase the food journey: from sourcing fresh and high-quality ingredients to kitchen preparation, to the dish served at the table. You can share behind-the-scenes videos, photos of chefs preparing dishes, and stories about the origins of your dishes.

Another way to use storytelling for restaurants on social media is to tell the story of your establishment. You can talk about your passion for cooking, the family traditions you've inherited, the values, and the philosophy that guide your restaurant. This way, your customers will feel involved, more likely to return to your restaurant, and recommend it to friends and family.

In addition to your restaurant's story, you can also tell your customers' stories. Ask them to share their culinary experiences at your restaurant and post photos of the dishes they've tried. You can also organize contests and giveaways on social media to encourage your customers to share their stories and increase engagement with your brand.

Finally, you can use storytelling to promote special events and initiatives at your restaurant. You can create hype around a themed dinner, a tasting evening, or a special holiday menu. Tell stories about these events, share live photos and videos, and engage your followers on social media.

Furthermore, it's important to use a variety of social media platforms to spread your storytelling. You can use Instagram to share high-quality photos and videos of your dishes, Facebook to tell longer and engaging stories, Twitter to interact in real-time with your followers, and LinkedIn to promote events and initiatives at your restaurant.

Lastly, remember that storytelling for restaurants on social media shouldn't just focus on food. You can tell stories about your restaurant's environmental sustainability, your social responsibility initiatives, and your partnerships with local producers. This way, you can build a stronger bond with your customers and differentiate yourself from the competition.

Storytelling for restaurants on social media is a powerful marketing tool that allows you to create emotional connections with your customers, increase engagement with your brand, and promote events and initiatives at your establishment. Use this technique creatively and strategically to stand out from the competition and increase your restaurant's online visibility.

15. Practical Tips for Achieving Success on Social Media with Your Business

The advent of social media has revolutionized how businesses market themselves, allowing them to reach a broader audience and interact directly with their customers. For restaurants, in particular, social media presents a huge opportunity to promote their brand, attract new customers, and retain existing ones. However, to succeed on social media, it's important to adopt an effective and consistent strategy. In this article, we will explore 40 practical strategies for achieving success on social media for restaurants.

1. Define your objectives: Before embarking on any social media marketing activities, it's important to have clear objectives. Whether it's increasing bookings, raising awareness of your brand, or boosting customer engagement, make sure you have clear and measurable goals.

2. Know your audience: Understanding your target audience is crucial for social media success. Conduct thorough research to understand who your ideal customers are, what they love, and what they look for in a restaurant.

3. Choose the right platforms: Not all social media platforms are suitable for every type of business. For restaurants, platforms like Instagram and Facebook are particularly effective for showcasing food images and engaging customers.

4. Create an editorial calendar: To maintain a consistent presence on social media and ensure a steady flow of quality content, it's important to create a detailed editorial calendar. Plan your posts in advance and ensure consistency in tone and messaging.

5. Leverage reviews: Reviews play a critical role for restaurants as they influence customer purchase decisions. Make sure to monitor

reviews closely and respond promptly to customer feedback, both positive and negative.

6. Create engaging content: To capture your followers' attention and differentiate yourself from competitors, create original, interesting, and engaging content. Experiment with different formats such as photos, videos, and stories to see what resonates best with your audience.

7. Use relevant hashtags: Hashtags are a great way to increase the visibility of your social media posts. Use relevant and trending hashtags to ensure your content is discovered by a wider audience.

8. Collaborate with influencers: Collaborating with influencers can help you reach a larger audience and increase your restaurant's visibility on social media. Look for influencers who align with your brand values and can help you achieve your marketing

goals.

9. Offer exclusive promotions: Promotions and discounts are a great way to incentivize customers to visit your restaurant and engage with your social media page. Offer exclusive specials and promotions for your followers to stimulate engagement.

10. Host contests and giveaways: Contests and giveaways are excellent ways to engage your followers and increase your restaurant's visibility on social media. Organize creative and engaging contests that encourage your followers to interact with your page.

11. Post consistently: To maintain a steady presence on social media and keep your followers engaged, it's important to post quality content regularly. Find a balance between the quantity and quality of your posts to maintain your followers' attention.

12. Use scheduling tools: To streamline the content publishing process and maintain a consistent social media presence, use scheduling tools like Hootsuite or Buffer to plan your posts in advance.

13. Monitor engagement metrics: Constantly monitor engagement metrics such as likes, comments, and shares to understand which types of content resonate best with your audience and adjust your strategy accordingly.

14. Optimize your profile: Make sure to optimize your social media profile with complete and up-to-date information about your restaurant, including address, opening hours, and contact details. Also, add an accurate description of your restaurant and a link to your website.

15. Invest in paid advertising: Paid advertising campaigns on social media can help you reach a wider audience and increase your restaurant's visibility. Invest in targeted ads to

promote your products and services.

16. Create a storytelling strategy: Storytelling is a powerful marketing tool on social media that allows you to emotionally connect with your audience and build a stronger bond with your customers. Tell authentic and engaging stories about your restaurant to capture your followers' attention.

17. Host special events: Special events are a great way to promote your restaurant on social media and attract new customers. Organize themed events, tastings, or special menus for holidays to create buzz around your brand and generate interest among your followers.

18. Respond promptly to messages: Make sure to respond promptly to messages and comments from your followers to show them that you care about their feedback and experience. Maintain a professional and friendly tone in your responses.

19. Collaborate with other local restaurants and businesses: Collaborating with other local restaurants and businesses can help you increase your restaurant's visibility on social media and expand your network. Look for synergistic partnerships that can bring mutual benefits.

20. Curate your profile's aesthetics: The aesthetics of your social media profile are crucial for creating a positive first impression on your followers. Ensure you use a consistent and eye-catching design for your profile, including high-quality images and a recognizable visual tone.

21. Engage your team: Involve your team in managing your social media presence to create a sense of ownership and engagement. Ask staff members to contribute ideas and content to make your social media presence more authentic and genuine.

22. Partner with food bloggers and critics:

Partnering with food bloggers and critics can help you garner positive reviews and generate buzz around your restaurant on social media. Invite food bloggers and critics to visit your restaurant and sample your dishes for visibility and credibility.

23. Share behind-the-scenes content: Sharing behind-the-scenes glimpses of your restaurant on social media is a great way to engage your followers and show them the human and authentic side of your business. Showcase the process of preparing your dishes, behind-the-scenes work, and stories from your team to create an emotional connection with your customers.

24. Create educational content: In addition to promoting your dishes and services, create educational and informative content to educate your followers about culinary trends, local products, and gastronomic traditions. Educational content can help position you as an expert in the industry and generate interest among your followers.

25. Cross-promote: Collaborate with other restaurants and local businesses for cross-promotion on social media. Leave comments and shares on your partners' posts to increase your restaurant's visibility and generate mutual interest among your followers.

26. Create user-generated content: Involve your customers in creating user-generated content, such as photos and reviews of your dishes, to increase engagement and trust with your audience. Organize contests and campaigns that encourage your followers to share user-generated content to boost your restaurant's visibility on social media.

27. Host online tastings and special events: Host online tastings and special events to engage your followers and offer them a unique and engaging gastronomic experience. Use live streaming platforms like Facebook Live and Instagram Live to interact directly with your followers and offer them a unique and engaging experience.

28. Consider creating a social group: Create a dedicated social group for your restaurant to engage your most loyal customers and create an online community around your brand. Use the group to share news, promotions, and exclusive content, and to interact directly with your customers.

29. Use social media analytics tools: Constantly monitor the performance of your social media presence using available analytics tools such as Facebook Insights and Instagram Analytics. Analyze key metrics such as engagement, reach, and web traffic to understand what works and how to improve your social media marketing strategy.

30. Experiment with geo-targeted advertising: Use geo-targeted advertising to target your local audience based on their geographical location and increase your restaurant's visibility among local users. Leverage geographic targeting features available on platforms like Facebook and Instagram to

reach a more targeted audience.

31. Create seasonal and thematic content:
Take advantage of holidays, celebrations, and seasons to create themed and seasonal content that grabs your followers' attention and generates interest around your restaurant. Create special menus, promotions, and events tied to holidays and seasons to engage your followers and boost engagement.

32. Implement social commerce: Utilize social commerce features available on platforms like Facebook and Instagram to allow your customers to order food directly from your social media profiles. Implement chatbots, interactive menus, and e-commerce functionalities to simplify the ordering process and increase online sales.

33. Improve image quality: High-quality food images are essential for capturing your followers' attention and stimulating their appetite. Make sure to use fresh, bright, and

well-composed food images to showcase your dishes and generate interest among your followers.

34. Partner with local influencers: Collaborate with local influencers and micro-influencers to increase your restaurant's visibility among the local audience and generate interest in your brand on social media. Partner with influencers who have a strong local presence and can recommend your restaurant to their followers.

35. Offer exclusive content for your followers: Create exclusive and special content for your followers to encourage engagement and customer loyalty. Offer your followers previews, discounts, and exclusive promotions to reward their loyalty and encourage them to interact with your brand on social media.

36. Monitor industry trends: Stay updated on culinary industry trends and food world news to create relevant and current content for your

followers. Use trend monitoring tools and follow industry influencers and bloggers to stay informed about the latest news and trends.

37. Collaborate with professional photographers and videographers: Invest in creating high-quality content to promote your restaurant on social media. Collaborate with professional photographers and videographers to produce high-quality photos and videos that highlight your dishes and environment.

38. Host online tasting events: Host online tasting events to engage your followers and offer them a unique and engaging gastronomic experience. Use live streaming platforms to broadcast live events where your chefs prepare special dishes and share exclusive recipes with the audience.

39. Focus on customer experience: Ensure you provide an extraordinary experience to your customers both online and offline to increase

customer loyalty and generate positive buzz around your restaurant on social media. Pay attention to every detail, from hospitality to service, to ensure a memorable customer experience and stimulate positive word-of-mouth among your customers.

40. Maintain authentic and transparent communication: Finally, make sure to maintain authentic and transparent communication with your followers on social media. Be genuine, answer questions clearly and transparently, and share genuine feedback to build a trusting relationship with your customers and promote your online reputation.

Success on social media for restaurants depends on a combination of effective strategies, creativity, and consistency in communication. By following the practical tips and strategies described in this article, you can increase your restaurant's visibility on social media, attract new customers, and retain existing ones. Maximize the potential of social media to promote your restaurant and create a lasting emotional connection with your target audience.

Index

1.Introduction pg.4

2.Goals to Achieve Through Social Media pg.15

3.Creating a Social Media Profile pg.19

4.Profile Optimization pg.27

5.Content Creation - Types of Content to Share (Food Photos, Menu, Special Events, Offers) pg.31

6.Use of Hashtags and Geotags to Increase Visibility pg.36

7.User Engagement - Responding to Comments and Messages pg.41

8.Collaborations with Influencers and Bloggers pg.46

9.How to Advertise: Pay-Per-Click and Pay-Per-Thousand Views pg.54

10.Performance Monitoring pg.63

11.Evaluating the Effectiveness of Adopted Strategies and Making Necessary Adjustments pg.68

12.Review Management pg.74

13.Following New Social Media Trends and Adapting Your Strategy Accordingly pg.78

14.Storytelling for Restaurants pg.83

15.Practical Tips for Achieving Success on Social Media with Your Business pg.87